GEORGE
WASHINGTON

Troll Associates

GEORGE WASHINGTON

by Keith Brandt
Illustrated by Hal Frenck

Troll Associates

Library of Congress Cataloging in Publication Data

Brandt, Keith, (date)
  George Washington.

  Summary: A brief biography of the first president of
the United States.
    1. Washington, George, 1732-1799—Juvenile literature.
2. Presidents—United States—Biography—Juvenile litera-
ture. [1. Washington, George, 1732-1799. 2. Presidents]
I. Frenck, Hal, ill. II. Title.
E312.66.B67   1985   973.4'1'0924 [B] [92]   84-8624
ISBN 0-8167-0256-X (lib. bdg.)
ISBN 0-8167-0257-8 (pbk.)

"First in war, first in peace, first in the hearts of his countrymen." That is the way George Washington was seen by those who knew him. And that is the way he has been remembered by the many generations of Americans who have lived since the days of the American Revolution.

More than anyone else, George Washington symbolizes the strength and courage that carried the Colonies through the Revolution to independence. And that same strength helped the new United States of America to prosper and grow.

George Washington was born at Pope's

Creek in Westmoreland County, Virginia, on February 22, 1732. The Washingtons were well-to-do farmers with property in many parts of the Virginia Colony. Three years after George's birth, the family moved to Little Hunting Creek Farm, another of their properties.

George's older brother, Lawrence, would later inherit this property and rename it Mount Vernon. And it was here that George Washington would one day settle down.

But in 1738, when George was not quite seven years old, his father, Augustine, decided that the family should move again. Their new home was at Ferry Farm. It was near an iron mine and foundry owned by Mr. Washington.

Until the move to Ferry Farm, George had not been inside a schoolroom. The Washingtons had always lived too far from any school for George to attend. Although he had received no formal education, George had learned to ride a pony, shoot a rifle, and help out on the farm.

Now, however, it was time for him to learn to read, write, and do arithmetic. So George was enrolled in a one-room schoolhouse run by the Reverend James Marye. It was in Fredericksburg, Virginia, across the Rappahannock River from Ferry Farm.

In the seven years George attended school, he learned to read and write well, though his spelling was less than perfect. Yet right from the beginning, he excelled at arithmetic. George had an orderly mind, and the logic of numbers appealed to him. Throughout his life, George kept clear, accurate, and complete records of his income, expenses, and other financial matters.

As much as George liked school, it did not take up all of his time. He became a superb horseman, marksman, and athlete.

When George was eleven, his father died. Mr. Washington left many properties to his children, and Mrs. Washington felt that George should prepare himself to be a farmer. So George was sent to stay with Lawrence at Mount Vernon.

Lawrence taught George about planting, managing the farm, harvesting and selling crops, and dozens of other important aspects of farming. He also introduced George to many influential Virginians.

When George was fifteen he met Lord Fairfax, a wealthy and powerful Virginia landowner. Fairfax liked the quiet, intelligent teenager. He was impressed that George had taught himself to use his father's surveying tools and to draw maps.

This gave Lord Fairfax an idea. The Fairfax properties in America extended over the Blue Ridge Mountains and through the Shenandoah Valley. But they had never been properly surveyed. Fairfax proposed that young George accompany the master surveyor on an expedition to survey these lands. George readily took the offer.

The survey party left on March 11, 1748, and lasted thirty-three days. During that time, George kept field notes for the survey.

He guided horses across rivers, saw his first rattlesnake, shot a twenty-pound wild turkey, and paddled a canoe thirty-eight miles in one day.

The trip was very exciting; but more important, the experience changed young Washington's view of life. He had seen forests and rivers and mountains. He had discovered a world that stretched west farther than the eye could see. He had learned firsthand of the richness and vastness of his country. It shaped the way he thought and acted from then on.

Over the next five years, George worked as a surveyor of Culpeper County, Virginia. During this time he made his only trip out of the country, traveling to the British West Indies with Lawrence, who had become very ill. George also managed the family properties and joined the Virginia militia with the rank of major. This was the start of his military career.

The British and the French both wanted control of the lands west of the Allegheny Mountains. Each tried to get the Indians to side with them. And when Virginia's governor, Robert Dinwiddie, learned that the French were moving down into the Ohio Valley, he decided to send a group of militia to order the French to leave. Young Major Washington, who had been through the area on his surveying trip, was chosen to lead the party.

Washington completed the mission and returned with greater knowledge of the American countryside and advice for Governor Dinwiddie. Washington suggested that a fort be built where the Ohio and Allegheny Rivers meet. This is where the city of Pittsburgh, Pennsylvania, is now located. The governor took his advice, and Fort Duquesne was built.

Washington was now a lieutenant colonel in the militia. He was ordered to recruit troops to guard the fort and to take command of it. But before he reached the fort with the men under his command, the French destroyed it. After a number of skirmishes with the French, Washington returned to Virginia.

These military encounters taught
Washington several valuable lessons. He
learned how to keep his troops in order, how
to manage supplies and transportation, and
how to make use of the woods and other
natural surroundings in battle. Not long
after, Washington put this knowledge to use
as commander in chief of the Virginia
militia. Later, he would do so again, in the
military engagements of the American
Revolution.

In the years between wars, Washington
married Martha Custis, a young widow with
two children. The family settled at Mount

Vernon. Here, George enjoyed life as a successful farmer and country gentleman. He also served as a member of the Virginia legislature, known as the House of Burgesses.

As a member of the legislature, Washington was not as openly critical of England as his fellow Virginian, Patrick Henry, was. Even so, Washington believed that the Colonies should not allow themselves to be pushed too far by their British rulers. And as the tyranny of Great Britain increased in the Colonies, Washington began to favor a move toward independence.

While he was a delegate to the first Continental Congress, in 1774, Washington did not speak out very often. But his military knowledge, steadiness, and intelligence impressed the other delegates. So it was no surprise when, a year later, the second Continental Congress elected him commander in chief of the army of the Colonies. Washington accepted the position and immediately set out to assemble an army.

The years of the American Revolution, beginning in 1775 and ending eight years later, in 1783, were difficult ones for the Colonies. They were especially difficult for the Continental Army. There were never enough supplies or rations for the troops. There was never enough money to pay the soldiers or to buy materials.

Without General Washington's patient and brilliant leadership, the Continental Army would most likely have fallen apart, and the Revolution would have ended in defeat for America.

But he wisely kept peace among his generals, lifted the morale of the weary and dispirited troops, and encouraged everyone to fight on after a series of losses to the British troops.

At the end of the war, a victorious Washington returned happily to Mount Vernon. He hoped to spend the rest of his life there. But a few years later, his country called on him again. The Articles of Confederation, binding the states together, were not working well. A new constitution was needed for the young nation.

Washington was asked to be president of the convention that would draw up this new constitution. As in the past, it was Washington's gift of leadership that held the convention together and brought the northern and southern states into agreement. These same qualities led him to be chosen as the first President of the United States of America.

George Washington served two four-year terms as President, from 1789 to 1793 and from 1793 to 1797. In those eight years, he appointed outstanding leaders to posts in his cabinet. Among them were Thomas Jefferson and Alexander Hamilton.

Under his direction, the United States government established a national mint and a sound banking system. And when federal troops put down a rebellion of farmers in Pennsylvania, it proved that the central government was strong and would enforce its laws.

The federal government under Washington made the first treaties with the Indians, admitted new states to the Union, and established a clear foreign policy. This policy was based on the idea that the new nation would observe good faith and justice toward all nations, but would remain neutral toward all of them.

George Washington felt strongly that the young United States needed time to grow, to solve its own problems, and to develop its vast territories. To do these things, he felt, the country had to stay clear of foreign entanglements.

In 1797, George Washington returned to Mount Vernon. There, he and Martha Washington enjoyed the most peaceful years of their marriage. Every day, the former President rode around his thriving estate, supervising the work. The Washingtons entertained friends and the many government officials who came seeking the great statesman's advice.

However, this happy retirement did not last long. In December 1799, George Washington became ill. And on December 14, the sixty-seven-year-old leader of the American Revolution died.

Following a military funeral, he was buried on the grounds of his beloved Mount Vernon. There he lies today, across the Potomac River from the nation's capital, which was named in his honor. There have been many Presidents of the United States since George Washington, but none commands the respect, love, and honor given to the man who is justly called the "father of his country."